THE SIMPSONS XMAS BOOK

TRANSMUTATED BY MATT GROENING

TELEPLAY BY MIMI POND

Harper Perennial
A Division of HarperCollins Publishers

First paperback edition published 1992.

ISBN 0-06-096960-1

92 93 94 95 96 RRD 10 9 8 7 6 5 4 3 2 1

Art Direction: *Mili Smythe*
Design: *Peter Alexander*
Editor: *Wendy Wolf*
Design Consultant: *Kim Llewellyn*
Production Manager: *Bill Luckey*
Production: *Junichi Hirota, Thea Piegdon*
Typesetting: *Access Publishing, LA, CA*
Color Separations: *Magna Graphics*
Printing: *R. R. Donnelley and Sons*
Moral Support & General Counsel: *Susan Grode*

'Tis the night
of the Springfield Xmas Pageant,
And all through the town,
Only one family is
stirring...

...the Simpsons.

"Careful, Homer!"

"No time to be careful, Marge! We're late!"

SPRINGFIELD ELEM SCHOOL ANN CHRISTMAS PAG

The Simpsons trudge ever-so-lightly into the packed auditorium ...

♪ OH LITTLE TOWN OF BETHLEHEM...... ♪

"Excuse us... pardon us, excuse me..."

"Oops! Sorry!"

"Pardon my galoshes! Heh, heh..."

WATCH IT!!

HEY, NORMAN. HOW'S IT GOING? SO YOU GOT DRAGGED DOWN HERE TOO... HEH, HEH, HEH.

WHERE'S A PROGRAM? THERE'S NO PROGRAM.

WASN'T THAT WONDERFUL? AND NOW "SANTAS OF MANY LANDS," AS PRESENTED BY THE ENTIRE SECOND-GRADE CLASS.

FROHLICH WEIHNACHTEN. THAT'S GERMAN FOR MERRY CHRISTMAS. IN GERMANY, SANTA'S SERVANT RUPRECHT GIVES PRESENTS TO GOOD CHILDREN AND WHIPPING RODS TO THE PARENTS OF BAD ONES.

MERI KURIMASU. I AM HOTSEIOSHA, A JAPANESE PRIEST WHO ACTS LIKE SANTA CLAUS. I HAVE EYES IN THE BACK OF MY HEAD SO CHILDREN BETTER BEHAVE WHEN I'M NEARBY.

GASP!!

Lisa enters, with flames.

"Jingle bells,　*Batman smells,*　*Robin laid an egg.*　*The Batmobile*

broke its wheel,　*And the Joker*　*got awa—*　*AAUGHH!!!"*

DOESN'T HE SING LIKE AN ANGEL?

D'OH !!

The next night, the Simpsons enjoy another evening of warm family togetherness.

...EVERY YEAR, STUPID CORD... WHAT TH--?!!

Dec. 23

Dear friends of the Simpson family,

We've had some sadness and some gladness this year. Our little cat, Snowball, was unexpectedly run over and went to kitty heaven. But we bought a new little cat, Snowball II, so I guess life goes on. Speaking of life going on, Grampa is still with us, feisty as ever. Maggie's walking by herself. Lisa got straight A's. And Bart, well, we love Bart.

The magic of the season has touched us all.

MARGE! HAVEN'T YOU FINISHED THAT STUPID LETTER YET?!

Homer sends his love.

Happy Holidays,
The Simpsons

"All right, children, let's have those letters to Santa, and I'll send them to his workshop at the North Pole!"

"Oh please. There's only one fat guy who brings us presents around here, and his name ain't Santa!"

"A pony? Oh, Lisa. You've asked for that for three years and I keep telling you that Santa can't fit a pony into his sleigh. Can't you take a hint?"

"Let's see if Bart's a little more realistic...a tattoo?!"

"Yeah, they're really cool and they last the rest of your life!"

"If you want a tattoo, you'll have to pay for it out of your allowance."

"All right!" "Homer!"

"OK kids, get ready for the *deluxe and spec-tac-cu-lar* Simpson Holiday Light Show Display! Marge, turn on the juice!"

A few paltry lights blink on and off.

"Nice try, Dad."

"Hey Simpson; do you think this looks okay?"

IT'S TOO BRIGHT.

GEE!

WOW...

SUCK!

HO, HO, HO...

RY XMAS

fizz! plink! sputter...

"Go and get your money."

"Spill it, Marge. Where have you been hiding the Christmas money?"

"Oh, I have my secrets... turn around!"

The next morning, at the breakfast table...

"OK kids, who wants to go Christmas shopping?"

"I do!"

"All right, the mall!"

OOOOHHHH!

"Ooh, big jar this year!"

THE H
TAT

XMAS
SPECIAL
UP TO 12
LETTERS
ONLY $15.95
The Perfect Gift!

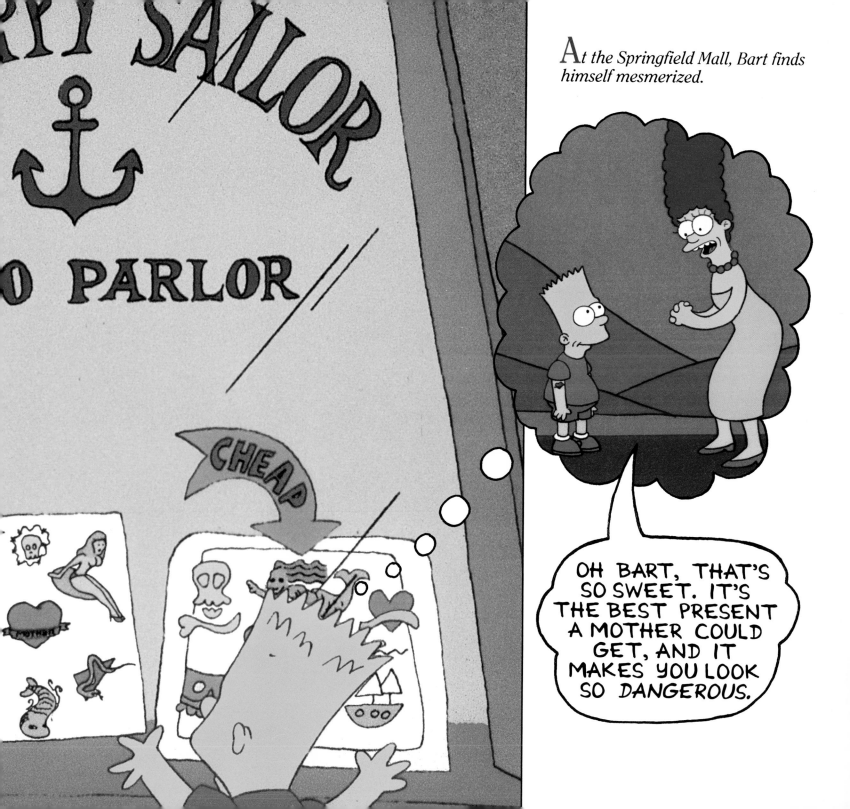

At the Springfield Mall, Bart finds himself mesmerized.

OH BART, THAT'S SO SWEET. IT'S THE BEST PRESENT A MOTHER COULD GET, AND IT MAKES YOU LOOK SO DANGEROUS.

B*art enters the tattoo parlor.*

 "One 'mother' please."

"How old are you?"

 "Twenty-one, sir."

"OK, get in the chair."

Meanwhile, over at the Springfield Nuclear Power Plant...

Back at the mall, Marge is troubled...

"Now, where's that Bart gotten to?"

"GASP!!"

"But Mom, I thought you'd like it!"

"Why would I like a tattoo that says 'Moth'?"

TATOO PAR

XMAS
SPECIAL
UP TO 12
LETT

*M*arge drags Bart to
*Dr. Zitsofsky's Dermatology
Clinic.*

"Yes, Mrs. Simpson, we can
remove your son's tattoo. It's a simple
routine involving lasers."

"Cool!"

"However, it is rather expensive
and we must insist on a cash
payment up front."

*T*hat night, Homer inspects Bart's bandaged arm.

"What's this?"

"It used to be a real boss tattoo—"

"—but Mom had to spend all the Christmas money to have it surgically removed."

AHGGH!

OH NO! IT'S TRUE!

WE'RE RUINED!

NO PRESENTS FOR ANYONE!

"Don't worry, Homer—we'll just stretch your Christmas bonus even further this year!"

"YAAAAAAAA!!"

"Homer?"

"Oh yeah, my Christmas bonus. Heh heh! How silly of me. This'll be the best Christmas yet. The best any family ever had! Heh heh! Ho! Ho! Ho!"

CHRISTMAS IS CANCELLED!!

*H*omer decides he'll buy
the presents.

"Well, if I do the Christmas shopping, no one will know about my
bonus. Now, let's see. Marge, Marge,
Marge...Oooh, look! Panty hose.
Practical and alluring. And a six-pack
is only $4.99...

OOOH, LOOK!

Oooh, pads of paper. I bet Bart can
think of a million things to do with
these...That just leaves little Maggie...
Oh look, a little squeak-toy. Says it's
for dogs, but she can't read..."

"And for me, some breath mints...
which the family will appreciate too."

"This is going to be a great...a ter-
rific...a...oh, who am I trying to kid!
This is going to be a rotten Christmas
and it's all my fault."

*S*oon, over at Moe's tavern...

"Whatzamattah, Homer? Somebody leave a lump of coal in your stocking? You've been sucking on that beer all day. It's Christmas—have a candy cane."

"What's with the crazy getup, Barn?"

"I got me a part-time job working as a Santa down at the Mall."

"Wow! Could I do that, too?"

"I don't know, they're pretty selective..."

BUURRP!!

At Santa School...

 "Now, before we send you out into the world, we require that you successfully complete our training program. Repeat after me: 'Ho ho ho. Ho ho ho. Ho ho ho.' "

HO HO HO!!
HO HO HO!!
HO HO HO!!

 "When do we get paid?"

"Not a dime till Christmas Eve. Now take it from the top."

"Ho ho ho. Ho ho ho."

"Hmmhmmm."

"Prancer, Nixon—"

"Mmmhmm."

"Comet, Cupid...Donna Dixon?"

"Sit down, Simpson."

COMET, CUPID...
DONNA DIXON?

HMPH!

HMPH!

"All right, Simpson. It's your turn to recite the names of Santa's reindeer."

"Dasher, Dancer—"

Very, very late the next night, Homer struggles home.

 "Oh, Hom—"

"Not a word, Marge. I'm heading straight for the tub."

"Oh, Dad, you're finally home!"

"Dad, we're so glad to see you!"

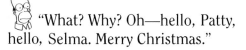 "What? Why? Oh—hello, Patty, hello, Selma. Merry Christmas."

"Oh, Patty, it's Christmas? You'd never know it around here... there's not even a Christmas tree."

"So, what do you think, kids? Beauty, isn't it?"

"Way to go, Dad!"

"Why is there a birdhouse in it?"

"That's an ornament."

Homer reports for duty...

> AND THEN I WANT SOME ROBOTOIDS, AND A GOOP MONSTER, AND A GREAT BIG GIANT--

"Ah, son, you don't need all that junk. I'm sure you've already got something much more important—a decent home and a loving father who would do anything for you! Hey--I didn't get lunch. Can I have a bite of that donut?"

Bart and his pals Milhouse and Lewis watch the action.

"I can't believe those kids are falling for it!"

"Hey, Milhouse, I dare you to sit on his lap!"

"Yeah, well, I dare you to yank his beard off."

"Ah, touché!"

Bart climbs on Santa's lap.

"Hey Santa, what's shakin'?"

"What's your name, Bart--er--little partner?"

"I'm Bart Simpson. Who the hell are you?"

 "I'm jolly old Saint Nick."

"Oh yeah? We'll just see about that!"

HOMER!!

"A word with you in Santa's workshop, little *boy*. Cover for me, Elfy?"

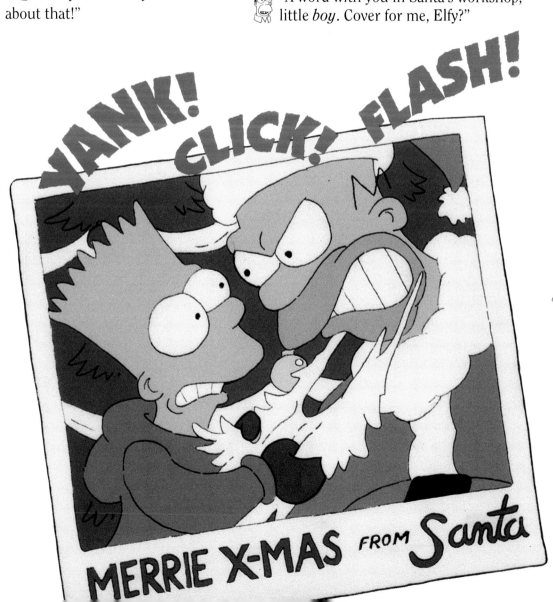

YANK! CLICK! FLASH!

MERRIE X-MAS FROM Santa

"Don't kill me, Dad. I didn't know it was you!"

"Nobody knows—it's a secret. I didn't get my bonus this year, but to keep the family from missing out on Christmas, I'd do anything."

"I'll say, Dad. You must really love us to stoop so low."

"Let's—sob—not get mushy, son —sniff—I still have a job to do!"

Finally, quitting time down at Santa's workshop. Bart and Homer stand in line at the personnel office, waiting for Homer's paycheck.

"Son, one day you're gonna know the satisfaction of payday—receiving a big fat check for a job well done. Let's go cash this baby and get presents for—THIRTEEN BUCKS?!!"

DEC 24

HOMER SIMPSON $13.00

THIRTEEN DOLLARS AND 00/XX

"That's right. One hundred and twenty dollars gross, less social security—"

YEAH--

"—unemployment insurance, Santa training—"

BUT-

"—costume purchase, beard rental, and Christmas club."

WAIT A MINUTE!

"Come on, Dad, let's go home."

"But we can't get anything for thirteen bucks!"

"All right! Thirteen big ones! Springfield Downs, here I come! I got a hot little puppy in the fourth race. Wanna come?"

"Sorry, Barney. I may be a total washout as a father, but I'm not going to take my son to some sleazy dog track on Christmas eve."

"Come on, Simpson. The dog's name is Whirlwind. Ten to one shot. Money in the bank!"

"Huh uh."

WHERE'S YOUR HUSBAND?

HE SAID HE WENT CAROLING WITH BART.

WE'RE IN THE MONEY! WE'RE IN THE MONEY!

"Come on, Dad! This can be the miracle that saves the Simpsons' Christmas. If TV has taught me anything, it's that miracles always happen to poor kids at Christmas. It happened to Tiny Tim, it happened to Charlie Brown, it happened to the Smurfs, and it's going to happen to us!"

"Well, okay...Let's go. Who's Tiny Tim?"

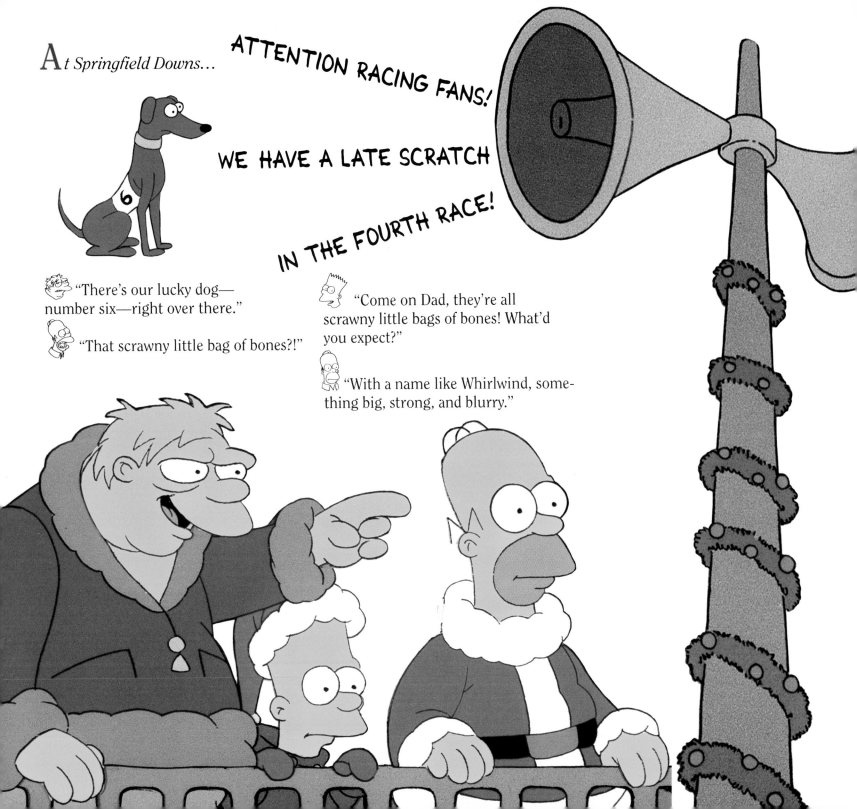

A*t Springfield Downs…*

ATTENTION RACING FANS!

WE HAVE A LATE SCRATCH

IN THE FOURTH RACE!

"There's our lucky dog—number six—right over there."

"That scrawny little bag of bones?!"

"Come on Dad, they're all scrawny little bags of bones! What'd you expect?"

"With a name like Whirlwind, something big, strong, and blurry."

NUMBER EIGHT, SIR GALAHAD, WILL BE REPLACED BY TA'S LITTLE HELPER!

 "Did you hear that? What a name! It's a sign! It's an omen!"

"It's a coincidence, Dad."

"What are the odds on Santa's Little Helper?"

"Ninety-nine to one."

 "Whoa! Ninety-nine times thirteen equals Mer-ry Christmas!"

"I got a bad feeling about this..."

"Don't you believe in me, son?"

 "Uh..."

 "Come on, boy—sometimes your faith is all that keeps me going!"

"Oh, go for it, Dad."

"That's my boy! Everything on Santa's Little Helper!"

 "All thirteen bucks?!"

*M*eanwhile, back home...

"These reruns get more boring every year."

"Where's Homer? It's past nine o'clock. This should be a time of family togetherness and joy."

"Typical of the big doofus to spoil it all."

"What, Aunt Patty?"

"Oh nothing, dear, I'm just deriding your father as a man."

TYPICAL OF THE BIG DOOFUS TO SPOIL IT ALL.

I WISH YOU WOULDN'T BECAUSE ASIDE FROM THE FACT THAT HE HAS THE SAME FRAILTIES AS ALL HUMAN BEINGS, HE'S THE ONLY FATHER I HAVE. THEREFORE HE IS MY MODEL OF MANHOOD AND MY ESTIMATION OF HIM WILL GOVERN THE PROSPECTS OF MY ADULT RELATIONSHIPS. SO I HOPE YOU BEAR IN MIND THAT ANY KNOCK AT HIM IS A KNOCK AT ME AND I'M FAR TOO YOUNG TO DEFEND MYSELF AGAINST SUCH ONSLAUGHTS.

"Mmmhmm. Go on and watch your cartoon show, dear."

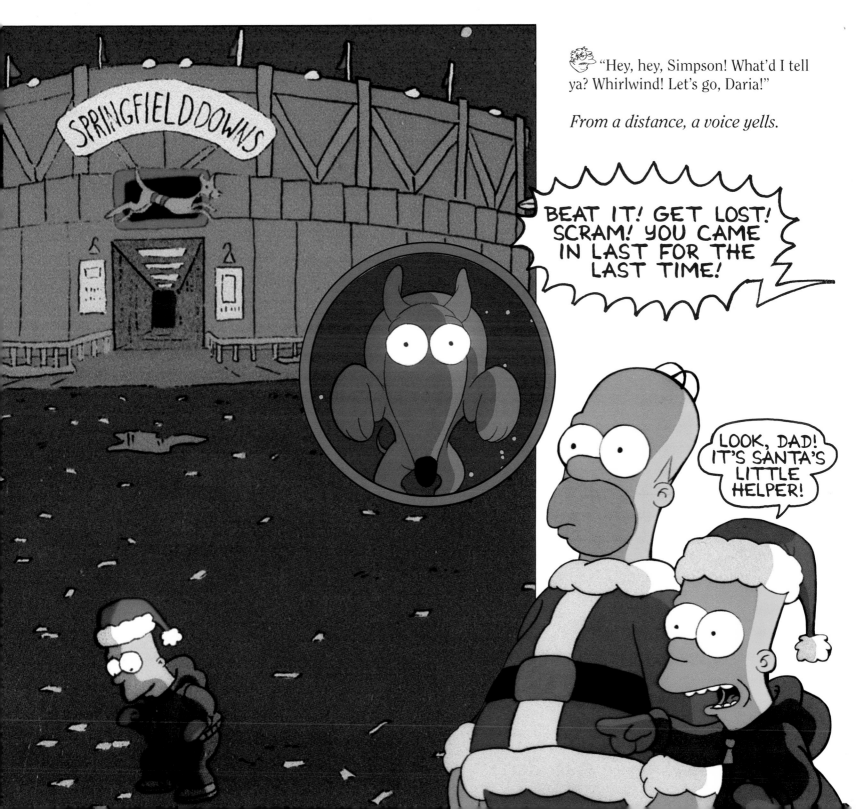

"Look, Dad, it's Santa's Little Helper!"

"Oh, no you don't!...no...no...! get away from me!"

The dog jumps into Homer's arms.

"Can we keep him, Dad? Can we? Can we?"

BUT HE'S A LOSER... HE'S PATHETIC... HE'S—

SLUURRRPP!

A SIMPSON.

*H*omer and Bart finally come home.

"DAD!"

"HOMER!"

"This should be good."

"Look everybody, I have a confession. I didn't get my Christmas bonus. I tried not to let it ruin Christmas for everybody, but no matter what I did, I just couldn't—"

"Hey everybody, look what we got!"

"A dog! All right, Dad!"

"This is the best gift of all, Homer, something to share our love—"

"It is?"

"—and frighten prowlers. What's his name?"

"Number eight. I mean, Santa's Little Helper."

And *they all hug happily, except for Patty and Selma.*

This book was adapted from the television show, "The Simpsons Christmas Special" (Copyright © 1989 by Twentieth Century Fox Film Corporation), first broadcast on December 17, 1989, a date which will live in infamy.

THE SIMPSONS

Created by .... MATT GROENING

Developed by .... JAMES L. BROOKS
MATT GROENING
SAM SIMON

Co-Producers .... LARINA JEAN ADAMSON
AL JEAN
MIKE REISS

Produced by .... RICHARD SAKAI

Written by .... MIMI POND

Directed by .... DAVID SILVERMAN

Executive Producers .... JAMES L. BROOKS
MATT GROENING
SAM SIMON

Starring .... DAN CASTELLANETA
JULIE KAVNER
NANCY CARTWRIGHT
YEARDLEY SMITH
and
HARRY SHEARER

Also Starring .... HANK AZARIA
JOANN HARRIS
PAMELA HAYDEN

Executive Consultant .... BRAD BIRD

Story Editor .... JON VITTI

Animation Produced by .... KLASKY-CSUPO, INC.

Supervising Animation Director .... GABOR CSUPO

Animation Producer .... MARGOT PIPKIN

Associate Producer .... J. MICHAEL MENDEL

Visual Consultant .... STEPHEN LINEWEAVER

Theme by .... DANNY ELFMAN

Music by .... RICHARD GIBBS

Casting by .... BONITA PIETILA

Script Supervisor .... LOUISE JAFFE

Production Coordinator .... SARAH WERNER

Production Mixer .... BRAD BROCK

Re-Recording Mixer .... GARY MONTGOMERY

Film Editors .... BRIAN K. ROBERTS
RIC EISMAN

Dialogue Editor .... BRIAN K. ROBERTS

Sound Effects Editor .... TRAVIS POWERS

Post Production Audio Facility .... TODD-AO/
GLEN GLENN STUDIOS

Post Production Facility .... LASER EDIT, INC.

Assistants to the Executive Producers
PATTY MacDONALD
JULIE STEDMON SMITH   DARIA PARIS

Assistants to the Producers .... LANA REPP LEWIS
STEVE GOTTFRIED
STUART BAKER
LESLIE RICHTER
MICHAEL McCUSKER
LISA STEWART

Post Production Coordinator ..... JOSEPH A. BOUCHER

Overseas Animation Director .... DON SPENCER

Animation Production Manager .... SHERRY ARGAMAN

Korean Production Company ...... AKOM PRODUCTION
COMPANY

Storyboard .... RICH MOORE

Character Design .... MATT GROENING
DALE HENDRICKSON
PHIL ORTIZ
SAM SIMON

Background Design .... ALVARO ARCE
PHIL ORTIZ

Layout Artists
BRONWEN BARRY   JANG WOO LEE
TIBOR BELAY   MICHAEL O'CONNOR
CULLEN BLAINE   EDUARDO OLIVARES
ZEON DAVUSH   GREG REYNA
STEVE FELLNER   SWINTON SCOTT
MILTON GREY   ERIC STEFANI
KARENIA KAMINSKY   MICHAEL SWANIGAN
GREGG VANZO

Main Title Design .... DAVID SILVERMAN

Main Title Animation .... KEVIN PETRILAK

Color Design &
Background Painting .... GYORGYI PELUCE

Assistant Film Editor .... DON BARROZO

On-Line Editor .... MARK McJIMSEY

Animation Checkers .... MAXINE MARKOTA
DOLORES HANSON
NIKKI VANZO

Animation Camera .... JIM KEEFER
WESLEY SMITH

Cleanup Artists .... NANCY KRUSE
DON JUDGE
JOE RUSSO

Production Assistants .... DONOVAN BROWN
TODD JACOBSEN
ELEANOR MILLS

Negative Cutter .... D & A NEGATIVE CUTTING

Executive in Charge of Production for Gracie Films
MICHAEL STANISLAVSKY

Executive Consultant .... SAM SIMON

Executive Creative Consultant .... JAMES L. BROOKS

A Gracie Films Production in association with
Twentieth Century Fox Television